The
Sweet, Still Waters
HOME
of

D0966584

The
Sweet, Still Waters
HOME
of

CAROL LYNN PEARSON

BONNEVILLE BOOKS
SPRINGVILLE, UTAH

ISBN 13: 978-1-59955-802-8

Published by Bonneville Books, an imprint of Cedar Fort, Inc.
2373 W. 700 S., Springville, UT 84663
Distributed by Cedar Fort, Inc., www.cedarfort.com

LIBRARY OF CONGRESS CATALOGING-IN-PUBLICATION DATA
Pearson, Carol Lynn.
  The sweet, still waters of home : inspiration for mothers from the
twenty-third psalm / Carol Lynn Pearson.
     p. cm.
   Summary: Inspirational essays that celebrate a mother shepherding her children as the Lord shepherds us all.
   ISBN 978-1-59955-802-8
   1. Mothers--Poetry. 2. Bible. O.T. Psalms XXIII. I. Title.
   PS3566.E227S94 2011
   811'.54--dc22
                                    2011001354

Cover and page design by Angela D. Olsen
Cover design © 2011 by Lyle Mortimer
Edited by Heidi Doxey

Printed in the United States of America

10 9 8 7 6 5 4 3 2 1

Printed on acid-free paper

Dear Lord my Shepherd,

I am a mother.
You have called me to assist you in
Shepherding a few dear lambs of the flock.

Their value is without price.
My abilities are imperfect.

Teach me to care for them as you care for us all.

I read the pattern of your perfect care
In the words of King David,
Royal shepherd of Palestine.

Help me to follow your lead.

1

The TWENTY-THIRD
PSALM *A Psalm of David*

The LORD is my shepherd; I shall not want.

He maketh me to lie down in green pastures:

He leadeth me beside the still waters.

He restoreth my soul:

He leadeth me in the paths of righteousness for his name's sake.

Yea, though I walk through the valley of the shadow of death,

I will fear no evil:

For thou art with me;

Thy rod and thy staff they comfort me.

Thou preparest a table before me in the presence of mine enemies:

Thou anointest my head with oil;

My cup runneth over.

Surely goodness and mercy shall follow me all the days of my life:

And I will dwell in the house of the LORD forever.

III

The
LORD
is my
SHEPHERD

The LORD *is my* SHEPHERD

This is not a question, my child.
It is a declaration.
The sheep do not have to audition for the shepherd
Nor do we.
The Lord *is* our shepherd!

I *am* your mother.
No ifs, no hidden clauses.
You are not here on approval.
I have received you into my fold and I will be there
With you
For you
Without conditions.

I am a given in your life and I am a gift
As are you.

You could decide to leave me
But I will never leave you.

1

And like the little story I read to you of the bunny that says
"I will become a bird and fly away"—
And the mother says
"Then I will be a tree that you come home to"—
I will always be there.

Should you become lost in the maze of this world
So full of deceptive paths and pitfalls
Like the good shepherd who leaves the ninety and nine
To go after the one who is lost
Even through the night and the storm,
I will search for you.

2

Should you lose the vision of
Who you really are
I will keep it alive
In the mirror of my eyes.

There will come a time when
The best mothering I can do is to stand back
And watch as you make your own way.

But even if we are separated by thousands of miles
My thoughts, my prayers, my hope
Will find you.

There is no distance between two points of love.

I am still your mother.

3

I SHALL
not WANT

I SHALL *not* WANT

"For want of a nail the shoe was lost.
For want of a shoe the horse was lost.
For want of a horse the rider was lost . . ."
And finally the kingdom was lost.

We have important needs, my dear one,
But they are few
Despite the clever commercials that
Declare our deficiency.
The Lord cares for us
And for the lilies of the field.

I would care for you in the same way
Supplying all you need to thrive.
I want you to want, my child,
But I do not want you to lack.

I will do all in my power to see that you have
Food that is healthy and tasty

5

A good warm coat every winter
A bed that is clean and comfortable
Walls and a roof that keep out rain and danger
Books that open hidden doors in your mind
Music that invites your soul to dance
Words from my lips that remind you always of your beauty
Hugs and back rubs
Love and laughter with all who are in our fold.

When your wants are not *lacks*
But your wants are *desires*—
They will take wing.

6

I will stand by and applaud
As did the mother of the child
Who wanted polio to be no more
Who wanted the slaves to be free
Who wanted the Berlin Wall to crumble
Who wanted marble to become the David
Who wanted to walk on the moon.

Carol Lynn Pearson

Ah, fed and clothed and loved
By the Lord and your mother
And the rest of the family
And good friends
What will you create, my child,
From the divine hunger in your soul?

He MAKETH *me to lie* DOWN *in* GREEN PASTURES

He MAKETH *me to lie* DOWN *in* GREEN PASTURES

Sheep are seldom still.
The shepherd starts them grazing about four in the morning.
By ten the sun is hot and the stomach of the sheep
Is full of undigested food.
So the shepherd makes the sheep lie down in a green pasture.
The sheep will not eat lying down
And so it reclines and chews its cud
And digests
And perhaps enjoys.

Those wonderful wants of yours, my child,
They need energy, ambition, drive.
But they need as well:
Relaxation
Silence
Peace.
Creativity thrives in stillness.

9

I would like to make of our home a green pasture
A place of rest.
I would like you to walk through the door and sigh
And feel some weight slip away
Because here is home and your spirit can lie down safely
Breathe more deeply.
You can digest your day.
You can dream of tomorrow.

I would like to learn how we can
Get Stuff Done Around Here
And still offer you a green pasture.

Green is the color of nature, fertility, life
Of growth, balance, harmony.

10

I will light candles.
I will bring in plants and flowers
And pillows.
I will sometimes play soft music
Even though it may annoy you

Because the sound is so different
From the sounds on your iPod.

There is time and room for it all
For grazing out there in the world
Gathering all that is nourishing—and then
Lying down in the green pastures of home.

11

He LEADETH *me beside the* STILL WATERS

He LEADETH *me* BESIDE *the* STILL WATERS

The shepherd leads
Walking confidently at the head of the flock
And the sheep follow.

The goal is to find still waters
For sheep will not drink
From waters that are turbulent.

The shepherd does not drive from behind
Forcing and frightening the herd.

I know that we seek to control
When we fail to inspire.
I have done that.
We yell, we spank, we push, we threaten.
Those are not still waters.

We encourage, we admire, we praise—

13

Our flock drinks deep and is refreshed.

You dress up, my child, in my things, in my words
And in my private thoughts.
There is no keeping my joy or my sadness from you.
My emotions are in the air between us
Like dust or oxygen
And you breathe them.

My peace takes you to still waters
My anger to troubled ones.

It is not easy to be the leader.

But wait.
I have remembered—a little child shall lead them.
Welcome thought!

There is so much I can learn from you
You with the wide-open eyes and the quick smile:
Delight, wonder, purity, laughter, curiosity, faith.

Let us take turns, then, in this dance

Carol Lynn Pearson

Of leading and following.

And if we keep our eye on
The Leader who never is lost,
Surely we will find and share
Those sweet, still waters.

He
RESTORETH
my SOUL

He RESTORETH *my* SOUL

I helped to create your body
My sweet child
But not your soul.
Your soul is the breath of God.

I am a watchman to your soul.
I see it soar
I see it sink.

And when the blows of this world
Take your godly breath away
When I read doubt or defeat in your eyes
When I see your soul suffer—

I will help restore it
With your favorite pie
With a joke
With an encouraging word:

"You are wonderful and you are beautiful
And you are loved."

"I am so proud of you."

"Yes, you can. Of course you can!"

"That is such good work."

"You are the best!"

Or perhaps, most powerful of all
I will just be still and listen.

And should you do things to damage your soul
I will help with the repair
Reminding you always of who you really are.

Even the psalmist David
Turned from his godliness and did wrong.
He was without strength and turned again to the Lord
Who restored his soul.

18

Out in the pasture, when a sheep unfortunately or foolishly
Finds itself on its back, feet in the air
It is a "cast" sheep.
It cannot right itself and will die if not noticed.
It is the shepherd's job to notice
To come to the sheep without blame or shame
And gently right it
Restoring it to its place in the flock.

I helped to give you life once, dear child of mine.
I will revive that life again and again.
I will be healer and friend to your soul.

19

He LEADETH ME *in the* PATHS *of* RIGHTEOUSNESS *for his* NAME'S SAKE

He LEADETH *me in the* PATHS *of* RIGHTEOUSNESS *for his* NAME'S SAKE

With several flocks at a watering hole
The time comes for leaving.
Each shepherd calls
And each sheep responds,
Separating itself out from the group,
Following the voice it trusts.

Sheep know the voice of their shepherd.

In Palestine the flock is always on the move
For the health of the sheep and the health of the ground.
And unlike many animals
The sheep has no sense of direction.
It cannot find its way home.
It needs the voice of its shepherd.
So many paths, so many cliffs.

You know my voice, my dear lamb.

You have heard it sharp when you ran into the street.

You have heard it sweet when I sang you to sleep.

You have heard it serious when I have called

"This way is safe.

This way leads to green pastures and still waters."

I wish to lead you only in right paths.

Even so

I know that my vision

Is not always perfect.

I know that "paths" is a plural word

And that your path will differ from mine

In wonderful ways

That I must encourage and celebrate.

I promise to remember

That my compass is not perfect

And that the only sure direction

In which I can point you

Goes not out there

22

But in here
Into that rich, private terrain of your heart
That kingdom of God within you.

Here
You hear the Lord's voice
The wise voice of your own soul
That still, small voice
That knows the way and leads you always
In right paths for his name's sake.

23

Yea, though I
WALK
through the VALLEY
of the SHADOW of
DEATH
I will FEAR
no EVIL

Yea, though I WALK *through the* VALLEY *of the* SHADOW *of* DEATH, *I will* FEAR *no* EVIL

Legend says that in the Holy Land there is a place called
"The Valley of the Shadow of Death."
It is south of the Jericho Road
Leading from Jerusalem to the Dead Sea
A mountain pass that shepherds named
Because of its steep sides, sheer rock walls
Caves and crevices that might hide animals of prey.

Grazing conditions made it a seasonal necessity
To move the sheep to the high country
Through this terrifying pass.

In our lives, my love, there is also
The Valley of the Shadow of Death
And unpredictably we are called there.
Walking that narrow path
We know darkness, disaster
Anxiety, loneliness, disappointment, anguish.

I have traveled through that place more than once.
The Lord my Shepherd was with me
As were friends who warmed me, walked with me
And kept me from looking down.

I know that you too will be called
To enter that demanding valley.
And I promise that you will not need to travel it alone.
The Lord our Shepherd will be with you.
I will be with you.
I will hold you, love you, weep with you
Protect and guide you as best I can.

And always, always, I will say to you—

26   "Child,

There is purpose to this path.
You have been *led* here.
Look up, not down.
This path leads to the high country
Where there is sun and clear water and birds
And the greenest of pastures."

Carol Lynn Pearson

Remember, my precious one
That it is only the *shadow* of death that we meet—
A dark pretender.

And remember too, we go *through* this dark valley.
We do not make our home here
Living on the ragged weeds
Of grief and resentment and fear.
We go *through* the valley, as sure-footed as we can
Reaching the high place of joy.

For THOU *art* WITH *me*

For THOU *art* WITH *me*

Did you notice?
Something remarkable happened in these five words.
"He" has become "Thou"!
The psalmist no longer speaks *of* the Shepherd
But *to* the Shepherd
As he does for the rest of the verse.

A heart, I think, broke open.
The Valley of the Shadow of Death will do that.

When the path is dark and narrow
Or a storm is raging
The sheep instinctively draws closer to the shepherd.
A new intimacy is born.
No longer "He," over there
But "Thou," here.
Here.

29

You and I will meet transformation too,
My most dear one.
Thunder will bring us closer.

After you have seen me weep
You will see me differently.

I will not always be the comforter.
There will be times when the strong arms
Will be yours
When the encouraging words
Will be yours
When the hand wiping the tears
Will be yours.

30   You will always see me as Mother.
But there will come a time
You will also see me as Friend
And I will see you as Friend.
I ask you now, Friend:

On my final journey
Through the Valley of the Shadow of Death—
Shepherd me.
Hold me and say:

"Mother.
There is purpose to this path.
You have been *led* here.
Look up, not down.
This path leads to the high country
Where there is sun and clear water and birds
And the greenest of pastures."

Thy ROD
and thy STAFF
they COMFORT *me*

Thy ROD *and thy* STAFF *they* COMFORT *me*

From ancient days
The shepherd has carried two things:
A rod, which is a club
And a staff, a long, slender stick with a hook on one end.

I carry these too, every day
And I pray to use them only for the comfort of my flock.

You have seen me use the rod, my dear
Never against you, never, never that.
But like the shepherd David who told King Saul
He used his rod to attack
The lion and the bear that came to raid his flocks
I have raised my rod against predators.

You have heard me say no to requests I consider dangerous
And to people I mistrust.
You have heard me say, clicking off the television,

"I did not invite these people into our home."
I keep vigil on the Internet
That vast unguarded terrain where wolves roam.

And this for your comfort.
I am on watch with my rod.

The staff is used for guiding sheep
Into a new path
Or along a dangerous and difficult route.
The tip is laid against the animal's side
With gentle pressure.

34

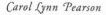

And when the sheep has lost its footing
And finds itself caught in brambles
Or in a crevice or a stream
The shepherd's staff becomes a long arm
And the hook a kind hand
To lift the helpless one to safety.

I hope for the wisdom to know
How much pressure to apply with the tip of my staff

Carol Lynn Pearson

Moving you toward those piano lessons
Or away from nose rings or tobacco
Or cheating on tests.

And I hope for the wisdom to know
When to rescue and when to stand back
When the bully in the playground appears
Or when you tell me at bedtime that you forgot
You need a costume for the program tomorrow
And here's the pattern for the pilgrim hat.

Thou PREPAREST *a* TABLE *before me in the* PRESENCE *of mine* ENEMIES

Thou PREPAREST *a* TABLE *before me in the* PRESENCE *of mine* ENEMIES

The high mountain country of the summer ranges
Was known as "tablelands."

Even before the snow had melted
The shepherd took great pains
To prepare this rough country for his flock
Plucking poisonous weeds by the root and burning them
Distributing salt and minerals
Clearing out the watering holes
Repairing small dams he made the year before
Tracking or trapping mountain lions
Or bears or other predators.

When he was finished—
A table prepared for his flock.

37

You graze at my table too, my dear
And I do my best to prepare it well—
Both the table of life
And the table in our dining room.

The one set for supper is the easiest.
I pluck and toss a lot of sugar and chemical sweeteners
Some meat
Partially hydrogenated vegetable oil
Foods processed to death
Leaving a spread of nourishment:
Whole grains, warm soup, fruits and vegetables of bright colors
Foods in proportion to the pyramid.

38

The table of life is more challenging to prepare.
I send you out daily to graze on lands
Over which I have little control.
I cast my vote, I write letters, I volunteer.
I crusade now and then
Against what I deem to be ignorance.
I point out to you the poisonous plants I cannot reach.

Carol Lynn Pearson

But here we are among enemies to life
Ideas and people who would rob us of our godliness.

I would not have you be afraid.

Even in the presence of those enemies
I ask you to go out with confidence
Into our beautiful world
Living by your best light.

And when you come in from the day
We will celebrate at the table I have prepared
Joyfully feasting on all good things
Frequently including chocolate,
Whose antioxidants bless body and soul.

39

Thou ANOINTEST *my* HEAD *with* OIL

Thou ANOINTEST *my* HEAD *with* OIL

At the first sign of flies, of parasites, of bramble scratches
Or injury of any kind to the head of the sheep,
The shepherd applies a balm, a remedy of olive oil
Often mixed with sulphur and spices—
Not unlike the anointing given to the traveler
By the Good Samaritan who poured oil into his wounds.

Immediately the troubled sheep becomes content.

I have anointed you often, my lamb
With lotion, hydrogen peroxide, sunscreen
Antibiotic ointment, calamine, lip balm
Various oils to protect and soften your skin.

But these are the mundane
Not the royal uses of oil.
I would that my blessing goes inches in
Past skin into soul.

I would anoint you, my honored guest
With customary oil poured upon your head
Anoint you to become the priest, the priestess
That you are in the Kingdom of God.

David was anointed King long before he became one.
I can do that for you.
I need no container or substance.
I anoint you with my vision
With my voice, my touch, my kiss.

I pledge to see you even in bad times
With eyes of charity
Through the mud and the mistakes
The failures (yours and mine)
The angry words, the bad grades
The rudeness, maybe even the tattoo (yours not mine)
See you as the anointed one
Dedicated to the service of God
The special one
A duplicate of which the world has never seen.

Carol Lynn Pearson

In Hebrew "messiah" means "the anointed one."
I anoint you with my anticipation
That your special gifts will help redeem this world.

I see you in advance of where your abilities presently are.
I hold the image of every good thing you are becoming.

I have authority.
I am your mother
And you are my anointed one.

My CUP *runneth* OVER

My CUP *runneth* OVER

After David brought his flock in for the night
And anointed the sheep's injuries with oil,
He dipped a cup into a large earthen jar of water
Bringing it out, never half full, but overflowing.

He then set it before a sheep
Who would sink its nose into the water
Clear to its eyes
And drink deeply until refreshed.

The Lord our Shepherd does that for us, you know
And his cup overflows.

We look at our lives and argue
Whether the cup is half empty
Or the cup is half full.

Wrong: the cup is overflowing.
I have learned that the only thing missing
From any situation is what I have failed to bring to it.

45

And I fail to bring only what I do not realize I have
For the Lord is my shepherd and I want for nothing.

And like the pot in the fairy tale
In which porridge overflows and pours onto the table
Onto the floor, out the door, into the village—
Or like the miraculous jar of oil that does not run out
For the widow who fed Elijah—
We have a source that never runs dry.

I would be as generous, my love.
I would be a mother who is never spent
Whose patience, kindness, wisdom, humor
Bubble over the brim.

But I am a cup that often feels empty
And my edges are sometimes dry and sharp.
Occasionally I am a desert.

Yet this I know:
The remedy for emptiness is appreciation.
When I find one thing about my life, about myself, about you

Carol Lynn Pearson

To appreciate, it invites another and another
And then, like magic, the cup expands and—
Such abundance:
Good measure, pressed down, shaken together,
And running over!

And this I can promise:
When I have little to give you
I will go to my Source and drink
Then meet a friend for lunch or for a walk
Read a chapter of a good book
Put on something I look pretty in
Add a little perfume
Notice what a good mother I am
And what a fabulous child you are
And spill some joy on you as you come in the door.

Surely
GOODNESS
and MERCY
shall FOLLOW *me*
all the DAYS
of my LIFE

Surely GOODNESS *and* MERCY *shall* FOLLOW *me all the* DAYS *of my* LIFE

Surely.
Not maybe, not probably.
Surely!

Just as sheep follow the shepherd
Because there is an affinity between them
So qualities and experiences and people follow us.

What we become sings its own song
Vibrates like a tuning fork
And is answered by its equal.

I would bathe you, wrap you
In goodness and mercy, my love.
I would feed you goodness and mercy
Fill our home with the sounds and smells and speech
Of goodness and mercy
Until they are in the soft marrow of your bones
And in your expectation.

49

Look for nothing else.

Do not wake up thinking that something bad is coming.
I know people whose creed seems to be:
Surely badness and harsh judgment will follow me
All the days of my life, especially today
And I'd be better off to stay in bed.

Know that you are followed, tracked, pursued
Not by enemies and persecutors
But by your best friends: goodness and mercy.

What I would teach you, child, I first must learn.

I must become a mother who bathes and wraps herself
In goodness and mercy.
Giving all to you and nothing to me
Is not good.
Forgiving you and finding fault with me
Is not merciful.

I must anoint myself with the oil of gladness
Dress myself in colors of praise

Carol Lynn Pearson

Serve myself from a full table
That I might have life more abundantly.

And when I forget or fail
Then mercy from you and mercy from me.

What a wonderful foursome we make
As we walk this path:
You, me, and the promised
Goodness and mercy that will follow us
Surely, surely
All the days of our lives.

51

And I will
DWELL
in the
HOUSE
of the
LORD
FOREVER

And I will DWELL in the HOUSE of the LORD forever

Such a journey this has been.
The Lord our Shepherd in the field
Is now our gracious host in his house
And we his honored guests
Not for one night of hospitality
But forever.

I have done the best I could
To provide a place for you, my child.
You dwelt first
In the small liquid house of my womb
Then outgrew it.
I have sheltered you
With strong walls and roof
And usually a room of your own
Decorated with posters of your own choosing.
You will outgrow these rooms as well.

But there will always be a bed for you at my house
And a place at the table.
Always.

There may be a time when you will offer me
A bed at your house
A place at your table.

And then—
That mansion on high we have heard of
Promised and held in escrow
It will be ours.

But I would give you the gift
Of living in the house of the Lord now.
Don't trade today for forever.

My motherly business is to build on holy ground
So you can become acclimated to love
Can use it as brick and mortar
For the home that you will make.

Carol Lynn Pearson

I am not a master builder
But I have a Master Architect and Teacher.
I can build a starter home
In the neighborhood of goodness and of mercy.

Here we will sing and laugh and learn
And smile and feast on good things
And forgive and bless.

Dedicated to the Lord, our house will become his house.
And when we change residence from our house to his,
Perhaps we will hardly know the difference.

We will dwell with him
On earth and in heaven
In the house of the Lord
Today and forever.

55